Campbell's

Fabulous One-Dish RECIPES

This edition is a revised and enlarged version of the **FAVORITE BRAND NAME RECIPES FABULOUS ONE-DISH RECIPES** cookbook.

This edition was produced by Campbell Soup Company's Publications Center, Campbell Soup Company, Campbell Place, Camden, NJ 08103-1799.

Corporate Editor: Pat Teberg

Assistant Editors: Alice Joy Carter, Margaret Romano

Creative Director: Stacy-Jo Mannella

Campbell Kitchens: Nancy DeBenedetta

Senior Marketing Manager: Brent Walker

Public Relations Manager: Kevin Lowery

Photography: Sacco Productions Limited/Chicago

Photographers: Tom O'Connell, Peter Walters

Photo Stylists/Production: Betty Karslake, Paula Walters

Food Stylists: Donna Coates, Lois Hlavac, Carol Parik

Assistant Food Stylist: Moisette Sintov McNerney

This edition published by:
Publications International, Ltd.
7373 North Cicero Avenue
Lincolnwood, Illinois 60646

ISBN: 0-7853-0078-3

Pictured on the front cover: Spanish Chicken and Mushrooms (*recipe page 4*), Pepper Steak (*recipe page 32*) and Golden Corn and Broccoli (*recipe page 78*).

Pictured on the back cover: Three-Cheese Pasta Bake (*recipe page 54*).

Manufactured in U.S.A.

8   7   6   5   4   3   2   1

Preparation and Cooking Times: Each of these recipes was developed and tested in the Campbell Kitchens by professional home economists. The preparation times are based on the approximate amount of time required to assemble the recipe *before* baking or cooking. These times include preparation steps such as chopping; mixing; cooking rice, pasta, vegetables; etc. The fact that some preparations can be done simultaneously is taken into account. Preparation times of "tip" and recipe variations are not included. The cook times are based on the minimum amount of time required to cook, bake or broil the food in the recipes.

Bakeware, cookware and serving dishes courtesy of: Revere® Copper-Clad Stainless Steel Skillet (page 9); Nordic Ware® Advance Performance Cookware® Chef Style Sauté Pan (page 19); Corelle® Country Violets Livingware Platter (page 21); Foley® Hearthside® Sauté Pan (page 27); All-Clad® Cop-R-Chef™ Sautepan (page 29); Club® Supra Cast Aluminum Covered Fry Pan (page 35); Anchor Hocking® Brentwood Basket Baking Dish Set (page 41); Anchor Hocking® Presence Cruet (page 43); Corning Ware® French White® Oval Casserole (page 45); Corning Ware® Classic Black™ Oval Casserole (page 47); Anchor Hocking® Amber Oven Basics® Baking Dish (page 49); All-Clad® LTD Covered Saucepan (page 67); Nordic Ware® Advance Performance Cookware™ Dutch Oven (page 69); Club® Supra Cast Aluminum Covered Dutch Oven (page 71); and Corning Ware® Classic Black™ Round Casserole (page 93).

M'm! M'm! Good! Cooking Begins With Campbell's Soups

Fabulous One-Dish Recipes features a recipe just for YOU—a recipe that's *fabulous*, *easy* and *one dish*. Every recipe has its own beautiful, mouth-watering photograph so you'll know what the recipe looks like before you begin cooking. And, many of the great-tasting recipes come with easy tips that suggest simple additions like a splash of wine, smoked cheese, sun-dried tomatoes, fresh herbs or toasted nuts to create extra-special dishes perfect for easy entertaining.

Every delicious recipe begins with a special ingredient—a can or package of quality Campbell's soup. Cooking with Campbell's soup eliminates the need for extra ingredients *and* helps you streamline preparation steps. We've included dozens of tasty main-dish recipes ready to serve from the skillet or oven, such as Skillet Corn and Chicken. Other recipes need only the simple addition of cooked rice or noodles, such as colorful Pepper Steak. For some, such as hearty Pork Stew Mexicano, all you need to complete the meal is bread or salad. And, for a quick stir-together side dish, serve savory Cheddar-Broccoli Noodles.

No matter which recipe chapter you turn to, every recipe is EASY! From our Kitchens to yours, we give you these Campbell favorites—they're *M'm! M'm! Good!*

Campbell's Family of Cooking Soups

Fabulous Skillets

SPANISH CHICKEN AND MUSHROOMS

Next time, serve this chicken dish over cooked orzo, a tiny rice-shaped pasta that cooks in about 8 minutes. Also pictured on the front cover.

2 tablespoons olive *or* vegetable oil
4 skinless, boneless chicken breast halves (about 1 pound)
2 cups sliced fresh mushrooms (about 6 ounces)
1 can (11⅛ ounces) CAMPBELL'S condensed Italian Tomato Soup
½ cup water
2 tablespoons Burgundy *or* other dry red wine
    Hot cooked noodles
    Fresh parsley sprigs for garnish

1. In 10-inch skillet over medium-high heat, in *1 tablespoon* hot oil, cook chicken 10 minutes or until browned on both sides. Remove; set aside.

2. Reduce heat to medium. Add remaining 1 tablespoon oil to skillet. Add mushrooms and cook until mushrooms are tender and liquid is evaporated, stirring occasionally.

3. Stir in soup, water and wine. Heat to boiling. Return chicken to skillet. Reduce heat to low. Cover; cook 5 minutes or until chicken is no longer pink, stirring occasionally.

4. To serve, arrange chicken over noodles. Stir sauce and spoon over chicken. Garnish with parsley, if desired.

Makes 4 servings	Prep Time: 10 minutes Cook Time: 25 minutes

Tip Prepare Spanish Chicken and Mushrooms as directed above, *except* in step 3, add ¼ cup sliced *pimento-stuffed olives* with the soup. In step 4, sprinkle ¼ cup grated fresh *Parmesan cheese* over the chicken before serving. Garnish with parsley and additional pimento-stuffed olives, if desired. *(Pictured)*

Spanish Chicken and Mushrooms

HONEY–MUSTARD CHICKEN

   Risotto Verde (see recipe, page 82) *or* **hot cooked rice**
1 **tablespoon margarine** *or* **butter**
4 **skinless, boneless chicken breast halves (about 1 pound)**
1 **can (10¾ ounces) CAMPBELL'S condensed Cream of Chicken Soup**
¼ **cup mayonnaise**
2 **tablespoons honey**
1 **tablespoon spicy brown mustard**
   Coarsely chopped toasted pecans *or* **walnuts**
   Fresh parsley sprigs for garnish

1. Prepare Risotto Verde as directed. Meanwhile, in 10-inch skillet over medium-high heat, in hot margarine, cook chicken 10 minutes or until browned on both sides. Remove; set aside. Spoon off fat.

2. In same skillet, combine soup, mayonnaise, honey and mustard. Heat to boiling. Return chicken to skillet. Reduce heat to low. Cover; cook 5 minutes or until chicken is no longer pink, stirring occasionally.

3. To serve, arrange chicken over risotto. Stir sauce and spoon over chicken. Sprinkle with pecans. Garnish with parsley, if desired.

Makes 4 servings	Prep Time: 5 minutes Cook Time: 20 minutes

Tip Prepare Honey-Mustard Chicken as directed above. Cut 4 thin slices from 1 *orange;* set aside slices. Grate peel from remaining orange to measure ½ teaspoon. In step 2, add orange peel with the soup. In step 3, arrange orange slices and chicken over the risotto. *(Pictured)*

Honey-Mustard Chicken

CREAMY CHICKEN–BROCCOLI NOODLES

This five-ingredient main dish can also be prepared with Campbell's Golden Corn Soup.

2 packages (3 ounces *each*) CAMPBELL'S *or* RAMEN PRIDE Chicken Flavor Ramen Noodle Soup
1 can (10¾ ounces) CAMPBELL'S condensed Cream of Mushroom Soup
½ soup can milk
1½ cups cubed cooked chicken
1½ cups cooked broccoli flowerets

1. In 10-inch skillet, cook noodles according to package directions. Add seasoning packets; drain off most of liquid.

2. Stir in mushroom soup and milk. Add chicken and broccoli. Heat through, stirring occasionally.

Makes about 6 cups or 4 servings	Prep Time: 10 minutes Cook Time: 10 minutes

Tip Prepare Creamy Chicken-Broccoli Noodles as directed above, *except* substitute *half-and-half* for the milk. In step 2, add 2 tablespoons grated *Parmesan cheese* with the mushroom soup. In step 2, stir ½ cup quartered *cherry tomatoes* and 2 tablespoons chopped *fresh parsley* into the hot chicken mixture. Makes about 6½ cups. *(Pictured)*

Creamy Chicken-Broccoli Noodles

EASY SOUTHWEST CHICKEN

Chili powder, stewed tomatoes and garlic powder give a southwest accent to chicken breasts.

1 tablespoon vegetable oil
4 skinless, boneless chicken breast halves (about 1 pound)
1 can (10¾ ounces) CAMPBELL'S condensed Golden Corn Soup
1 can (about 8 ounces) stewed tomatoes, cut up
1 teaspoon chili powder
¼ teaspoon garlic powder
   Hot cooked rice
   Fresh parsley sprig for garnish

1. In 10-inch skillet over medium-high heat, in hot oil, cook chicken 10 minutes or until browned on both sides. Remove; set aside. Spoon off fat.

2. In same skillet, combine soup, tomatoes, chili powder and garlic powder. Heat to boiling. Return chicken to skillet. Reduce heat to low. Cover; cook 5 minutes or until chicken is no longer pink, stirring occasionally.

3. To serve, arrange chicken over rice. Stir sauce and spoon over chicken. Garnish with parsley, if desired.

Makes 4 servings	Prep Time: 5 minutes Cook Time: 20 minutes

Tip Prepare Easy Southwest Chicken as directed above, *except* in step 2, sprinkle ½ cup shredded *Monterey Jack cheese* (2 ounces) and 2 tablespoons finely chopped *green pepper* over the cooked chicken. Remove from heat. Cover; let stand 1 minute until cheese melts.

SKILLET HERB–ROASTED CHICKEN

*Lightly seasoned chicken breasts are quickly pan "roasted" and served
with a creamy sauce.*

2 tablespoons all-purpose flour
¼ teaspoon ground sage
¼ teaspoon dried thyme leaves, crushed
4 skinless, boneless chicken breast halves *or* 8 skinless, boneless
    chicken thighs (about 1 pound)
2 tablespoons margarine *or* butter
1 can (10¾ ounces) CAMPBELL'S condensed Cream of Chicken Soup
½ cup water
   Hot cooked rice *or* noodles
   Green onion, orange slice *and* fresh mushroom for garnish

1. On waxed paper, combine flour, sage and thyme. Coat chicken lightly
   with flour mixture.

2. In 10-inch skillet over medium-high heat, in hot margarine, cook
   chicken 15 minutes or until browned on both sides and no longer pink
   in center. Remove; set aside. Keep warm. Spoon off fat.

3. In same skillet, combine soup and water. Heat to boiling. Reduce heat to
   low. Cover; cook 5 minutes, stirring occasionally.

4. To serve, arrange chicken over rice. Spoon sauce over chicken. Garnish
   with green onion, orange slice and mushroom, if desired.

Makes 4 servings	Prep Time: 5 minutes Cook Time: 25 minutes

Herbed Chicken and Mushrooms: Prepare Skillet Herb-Roasted Chicken
as directed above, *except* in step 3, add 2 cups sliced *fresh white mushrooms*
(about 6 ounces) or sliced *fresh shiitake mushrooms* (about 4 ounces) with
the soup. Reduce water to *⅓ cup* and add ¼ cup *Chablis or other dry white
wine. (Pictured)*

Herbed Chicken and Mushrooms

SAVORY CHICKEN BREASTS

*This fast-to-fix entrée is made with Italian Tomato Soup that has pieces
of tomato and is seasoned with onion, basil, oregano and garlic.*

   2 tablespoons all-purpose flour
   ⅛ teaspoon pepper
   4 skinless, boneless chicken breast halves (about 1 pound)
   2 tablespoons vegetable oil
   1 can (11⅛ ounces) CAMPBELL'S condensed Italian Tomato Soup
   ½ cup water
       Hot cooked noodles
       Fresh thyme sprigs for garnish

1. On waxed paper, combine flour and pepper. Coat chicken lightly with
   flour mixture.

2. In 10-inch skillet over medium-high heat, in hot oil, cook chicken
   10 minutes or until browned on both sides. Remove; set aside. Spoon
   off fat.

3. In same skillet, combine soup and water. Heat to boiling. Return
   chicken to skillet. Reduce heat to low. Cover; cook 5 minutes or until
   chicken is no longer pink, stirring occasionally.

4. To serve, arrange chicken over noodles. Stir sauce and spoon over
   chicken. Garnish with thyme, if desired.

Makes 4 servings	Prep Time: 5 minutes Cook Time: 20 minutes

Savory Chicken and Shrimp: Prepare Savory Chicken Breasts as directed
above, *except* in step 3, add ¼ pound medium *shrimp*, shelled and
deveined, with the browned chicken and continue to cook until shrimp
are pink and opaque. *(Pictured)*

Savory Chicken and Shrimp

HUNTER'S CHICKEN

¼ cup all-purpose flour
1 teaspoon dried basil leaves, crushed
¼ teaspoon garlic powder
¼ teaspoon pepper
8 chicken thighs (about 2 pounds), skin removed
1 tablespoon vegetable oil
1 can (10¾ ounces) CAMPBELL'S condensed Golden Mushroom Soup
1 can (about 8 ounces) stewed tomatoes, cut up
1 small carrot, thinly sliced (about ⅓ cup)
1 medium zucchini, sliced (2 cups)
   Hot cooked noodles
   Grated Parmesan cheese

1. On waxed paper, combine flour, basil, garlic powder and pepper. Coat chicken lightly with flour mixture.

2. In 10-inch skillet over medium-high heat, in hot oil, cook *half* of the chicken 10 minutes or until browned on both sides. Remove; set aside. Repeat with remaining chicken. Spoon off fat.

3. In same skillet, combine soup, tomatoes and carrot. Heat to boiling. Return chicken to skillet. Reduce heat to low. Cover; cook 15 minutes, stirring occasionally.

4. Stir in zucchini. Cover; cook 10 minutes more or until chicken is no longer pink and juices run clear, stirring occasionally.

5. To serve, arrange chicken over noodles. Stir sauce and spoon over chicken. Sprinkle with Parmesan cheese.

Makes 4 servings	Prep Time: 10 minutes Cook Time: 40 minutes

Tip   Prepare Hunter's Chicken as directed above, *except* in step 3, add ¼ cup *Burgundy or other dry red wine* with the soup.

QUICK CHICKEN 'N' NOODLES

This hearty dinner-in-a-skillet can be made in less than 30 minutes.

1 tablespoon vegetable oil
4 skinless, boneless chicken breast halves (about 1 pound)
1 can (10½ ounces) CAMPBELL'S condensed Chicken Broth
¾ cup water
½ teaspoon dried basil leaves, crushed
⅛ teaspoon pepper
2 packages (3 ounces *each*) CAMPBELL'S *or* RAMEN PRIDE
    Chicken Flavor Ramen Noodle Soup
1 package (10 ounces) frozen peas and pearl onions
¼ teaspoon paprika

1. In 10-inch skillet over medium-high heat, in hot oil, cook chicken
    10 minutes or until browned on both sides. Remove; set aside. Spoon
    off fat.

2. In same skillet, combine broth, water, basil and pepper. Heat to boiling.

3. Return chicken to skillet. Add noodles and peas. (Reserve seasoning
    packets for another use.) Return to boiling. Reduce heat to low. Cover;
    cook 5 minutes or until chicken is no longer pink and vegetables are
    tender, stirring occasionally to separate noodles. Sprinkle paprika over
    chicken.

Makes 4 servings	Prep Time: 5 minutes Cook Time: 20 minutes

Tip   Prepare Quick Chicken 'n' Noodles as directed above, *except* in
step 3, add ¼ cup finely chopped *oil-packed sun-dried tomatoes* with the
browned chicken.

Quick Chicken 'n' Noodles

EASY CHICKEN PAPRIKASH

Spaetzle, a small German noodle-like dumpling, is sold two convenient ways: dried or frozen.

1 tablespoon margarine *or* butter
4 skinless, boneless chicken breast halves (about 1 pound)
1 can (10¾ ounces) CAMPBELL'S condensed Cream of Mushroom
  Soup
2 teaspoons paprika
⅛ teaspoon ground red pepper
  Hot cooked spaetzle *or* noodles
⅓ cup sour cream *or* plain yogurt
  Chopped fresh parsley
  Sliced cherry tomatoes *and* fresh parsley sprigs for garnish

1. In 10-inch skillet over medium-high heat, in hot margarine, cook chicken 10 minutes or until browned on both sides. Remove; set aside. Spoon off fat.

2. In same skillet, combine soup, paprika and pepper. Heat to boiling. Return chicken to skillet. Reduce heat to low. Cover; cook 5 minutes or until chicken is no longer pink, stirring occasionally. Arrange chicken over spaetzle. Keep warm.

3. Stir sour cream into mixture in skillet. Heat through, stirring constantly. *Do not boil.*

4. To serve, spoon sauce over chicken. Sprinkle chicken with chopped parsley. Garnish with tomatoes and parsley sprigs, if desired.

Makes 4 servings	Prep Time: 5 minutes Cook Time: 25 minutes

Chicken Paprikash with Vegetables: Prepare Easy Chicken Paprikash as directed above, *except* in step 2, add 2 tablespoons *dry white vermouth* and 1 package (10 ounces) *frozen peas and pearl onions* with the soup and increase cook time to 8 minutes or cook until chicken is no longer pink and vegetables are tender.

Easy Chicken Paprikash

SKILLET CORN AND CHICKEN

This deliciously easy recipe features Golden Corn Soup.

1 tablespoon margarine *or* butter
4 skinless, boneless chicken breast halves (about 1 pound)
1 can (10¾ ounces) CAMPBELL'S condensed Golden Corn Soup
½ cup milk
2 cups broccoli flowerets
½ cup shredded Cheddar cheese (2 ounces)
⅛ teaspoon pepper

1. In 10-inch skillet over medium-high heat, in hot margarine, cook chicken 10 minutes or until browned on both sides. Remove; set aside. Spoon off fat.

2. In same skillet, combine soup and milk. Add broccoli, Cheddar cheese and pepper. Heat to boiling, stirring occasionally. Return chicken to skillet. Reduce heat to low. Cover; cook 10 minutes or until chicken is no longer pink and broccoli is tender-crisp, stirring occasionally.

Makes 4 servings	Prep Time: 10 minutes Cook Time: 25 minutes

Tip Prepare Skillet Corn and Chicken as directed above, *except* in step 2, sprinkle with additional Cheddar cheese and toasted *sliced almonds* before serving. *(Pictured)*

Skillet Corn and Chicken

SPICY SHRIMP AND NOODLES

2 **cups water**
2 **tablespoons soy sauce**
1 **teaspoon ground ginger**
½ **teaspoon crushed red pepper**
¼ **teaspoon garlic powder**
2 **packages (3 ounces** *each***) CAMPBELL'S Oriental Flavor** *or* **RAMEN**
    PRIDE Chicken Flavor Ramen Noodle Soup
1 **pound medium shrimp, shelled and deveined**
1 **cup green onions cut in 2-inch pieces**
    Chopped fresh parsley, green onion brush, orange peel *and*
    lemon slice for garnish

1. In 10-inch skillet over high heat, combine water, soy sauce, ginger, pepper, garlic powder and *half* of *one* seasoning packet. Heat to boiling. (Reserve remaining 1½ seasoning packets for another use.)

2. Add noodles, shrimp and green onion pieces. Return to boiling. Reduce heat to low. Cook 5 minutes or until shrimp are pink and opaque and noodles are tender, stirring occasionally to separate noodles.

3. To serve, arrange mixture on platter. Sprinkle with parsley and garnish with green onion brush, orange peel and lemon slice, if desired.

Makes about 4½ cups or 4 servings	Prep Time: 10 minutes Cook Time: 15 minutes

Tip Prepare Spicy Shrimp and Noodles as directed above, *except* in step 2, add 1 cup frozen *Oriental-style mixed vegetable combination* with the noodles. Sprinkle with toasted *sesame seeds* before serving. Makes about 5½ cups.

Spicy Shrimp and Noodles

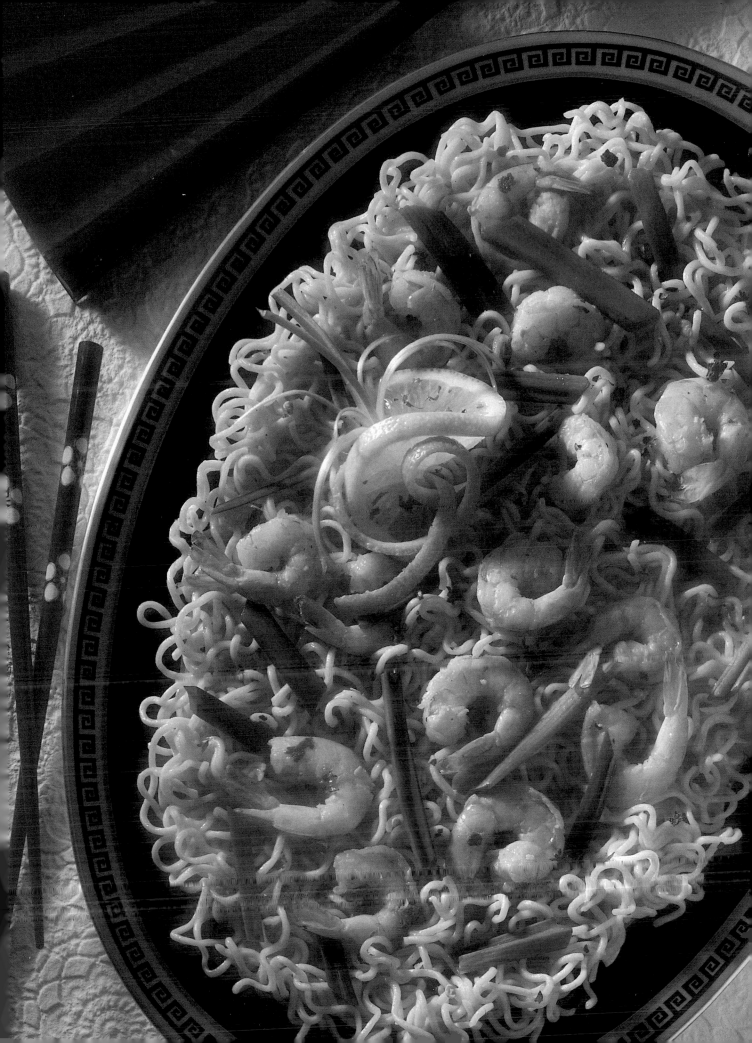

CHEESY TUNA AND NOODLES

Ramen Noodle Soup and tuna team together for a fast-to-fix one-dish supper.

   3 packages (3 ounces *each*) CAMPBELL'S *or* RAMEN PRIDE
      Chicken Flavor Ramen Noodle Soup
   2 tablespoons margarine *or* butter
   1 package (10 ounces) frozen mixed vegetables, thawed and drained
   1 clove garlic, minced
   1 can (10¾ ounces) CAMPBELL'S condensed Cream of Mushroom
      Soup
  ¾ cup milk
1½ cups shredded mozzarella cheese (6 ounces)
 ⅛ teaspoon pepper
   Generous dash ground nutmeg
   1 can (about 7 ounces) tuna, drained and broken into chunks

1. Cook noodles according to package directions. Add seasoning packets; drain off most of liquid. Set aside.

2. In 10-inch skillet over medium heat, in hot margarine, cook vegetables and garlic 2 minutes, stirring often.

3. Stir in mushroom soup and milk. Add mozzarella cheese, pepper and nutmeg. Cook until cheese melts, stirring occasionally.

4. Stir in reserved noodles and tuna. Heat through, stirring occasionally.

Makes about 7 cups or 6 servings	Prep Time: 10 minutes Cook Time: 15 minutes

Salmon Noodle Skillet: Prepare Cheesy Tuna and Noodles as directed above, *except* substitute 1 package (10 ounces) *frozen cut green beans,* thawed and drained, for the mixed vegetables and 1 can (about 7 ounces) *salmon,* drained and broken into chunks, for the tuna. In step 3, add 1 can (8 ounces) sliced *water chestnuts,* drained, with the cheese. *(Pictured)*

Salmon Noodle Skillet

SKILLET PORK AND RICE

Meaty pork shoulder chops and rice simmer in a delicate orange-flavored chicken broth.

1 tablespoon olive *or* vegetable oil
4 pork shoulder chops, each cut ¾ inch thick
1 cup regular long-grain rice, uncooked
½ cup chopped onion
1 can (10½ ounces) CAMPBELL'S condensed Chicken Broth
1 cup orange juice
3 tablespoons chopped fresh parsley
4 orange slices
  Fresh parsley sprigs for garnish

1. In 10-inch skillet over medium-high heat, in hot oil, cook chops 10 minutes or until browned on both sides. Remove; set aside.

2. In same skillet, combine rice and onion; cook 3 minutes or until lightly browned, stirring constantly.

3. Gradually stir in broth, orange juice and *2 tablespoons* of chopped parsley. Heat to boiling. Return chops to skillet. Reduce heat to low. Cover; cook 20 minutes or until liquid is absorbed and chops are no longer pink.

4. To serve, top each chop with orange slice and sprinkle remaining 1 tablespoon chopped parsley over orange slices. Garnish with parsley sprigs, if desired.

Makes 4 servings	Prep Time: 10 minutes Cook Time: 40 minutes

Tip Prepare Skillet Pork and Rice as directed above, *except* in step 4, sprinkle ¼ cup lightly salted *cashews*, coarsely chopped, over the orange slices.

Skillet Pork and Rice

HAM AND PASTA SKILLET

1 can (10¾ ounces) CAMPBELL'S condensed Broccoli Cheese Soup
1 cup milk
1 tablespoon spicy brown mustard
2 cups fresh broccoli flowerets *or* frozen broccoli cuts
3 cups cooked medium shell macaroni (about 2 cups dry)
1½ cups cooked ham cut in matchstick-thin strips (8 ounces)
   Red onion wedges for garnish

1. In 10-inch skillet, combine soup, milk and mustard. Over medium heat, heat to boiling.

2. Stir in broccoli. Return to boiling. Reduce heat to low. Cover; cook 5 minutes or until broccoli is tender. Stir in macaroni and ham. Heat through, stirring occasionally.

3. To serve, arrange mixture on platter. Garnish with onion, if desired.

Makes about 6 cups or 4 servings	Prep Time: 20 minutes Cook Time: 15 minutes

Chicken and Pasta Skillet: Prepare Ham and Pasta Skillet as directed above, *except* substitute 2 tablespoons *Dijon-style mustard* for the spicy brown mustard, 3 cups cooked *radiatore pasta* (about 2 cups dry) for the shell macaroni and 1½ cups *cooked chicken strips* for the ham.

Ham and Pasta Skillet

PEPPER STEAK

Ginger and soy sauce flavor the tender strips of beef and sweet peppers in this Oriental-style dish. Also pictured on the front cover.

2 tablespoons vegetable oil
2 cups sweet pepper strips (green, red and/or yellow)
1 medium onion, cut into 8 wedges
2 cloves garlic, minced
1 pound boneless beef sirloin steak, cut into thin strips
1 can (10¾ ounces) CAMPBELL'S condensed Beefy Mushroom Soup
1 tablespoon soy sauce
½ teaspoon ground ginger
Hot cooked rice

1. In 10-inch skillet or wok over medium-high heat, in *1 tablespoon* hot oil, stir-fry peppers, onion and garlic until tender-crisp. Remove; set aside.

2. In same skillet in remaining 1 tablespoon hot oil, stir-fry *half* of beef until browned. Remove; set aside. Repeat with remaining beef.

3. In same skillet, combine soup, soy sauce and ginger. Return reserved vegetables and beef to skillet. Heat through, stirring occasionally.

4. To serve, arrange rice on platter. Spoon mixture over rice.

Makes about 5 cups or 4 servings	Prep Time: 15 minutes Cook Time: 15 minutes

Tip Prepare Pepper Steak as directed above, *except* substitute 1 tablespoon *oyster sauce* for the soy sauce and 1 teaspoon grated *fresh ginger* for the ground ginger.

SKILLET BEEF 'N' NOODLES

This skillet supper can be made with condensed Tomato Soup, too.

2 packages (3 ounces *each*) CAMPBELL'S *or* RAMEN PRIDE Beef
    Flavor Ramen Noodle Soup
1 pound ground beef
½ cup chopped onion
1 can (11⅛ ounces) CAMPBELL'S condensed Italian Tomato Soup
½ soup can water
1 teaspoon Worcestershire sauce
1 teaspoon prepared mustard
    Generous dash pepper
    Fresh basil leaves, fresh oregano sprig, tomato slices *and*
    grated Parmesan cheese for garnish

1. Cook noodles according to package directions. Add seasoning packets; drain off most of liquid. Set aside.

2. Meanwhile, in 10-inch skillet over medium-high heat, cook beef and onion until beef is browned and onion is tender, stirring to separate meat. Spoon off fat.

3. Stir in tomato soup, water, Worcestershire, mustard and pepper. Stir in reserved noodles. Heat through, stirring occasionally. Garnish with basil, oregano, tomato and Parmesan cheese, if desired. Serve with additional Parmesan cheese, if desired.

Makes about 5½ cups or 4 servings	Prep Time: 5 minutes Cook Time: 15 minutes

Tip   Prepare Skillet Beef 'n' Noodles as directed above, *except* in step 3, add ½ cup *sour cream* with the noodles.

VEGETABLE–BEEF STIR-FRY

To make slicing the meat easier, freeze the beef about 1 hour
before cutting into thin strips.

   1 pouch CAMPBELL'S Dry Onion Quality Soup and Recipe Mix
  ¼ teaspoon ground ginger
  ⅛ teaspoon garlic powder
  ¾ cup water
   1 tablespoon vegetable oil
   1 pound boneless beef sirloin steak, cut into thin strips
1½ cups broccoli flowerets
   2 medium carrots, cut into matchstick-thin strips (about 1 cup)
     Hot cooked rice with chives

1. In small bowl, combine soup mix, ginger, garlic powder and water; set aside.

2. In 10-inch skillet or wok over medium-high heat, in hot oil, stir-fry *half* of the beef until browned. Remove; set aside. Repeat with remaining beef. Spoon off fat.

3. In same skillet, combine soup mixture, broccoli and carrots. Heat to boiling. Reduce heat to low. Cover; cook 3 minutes or until vegetables are tender-crisp, stirring occasionally.

4. Return beef to skillet. Heat through, stirring occasionally.

5. To serve, arrange mixture on platter. Serve with rice.

Makes about 4 cups or 4 servings	Prep Time: 15 minutes Cook Time: 15 minutes

Tip   Prepare Vegetable-Beef Stir-Fry as directed above, *except* substitute 1 teaspoon grated *fresh ginger* for the ground ginger.

SHORTCUT SLOPPY JOES

*For "Souper Pitas," spoon meat mixture into six pita bread halves and top
with shredded mozzarella cheese.*

1 pound ground beef
1 can (11⅛ ounces) CAMPBELL'S condensed Italian Tomato Soup
¼ cup water
2 teaspoons Worcestershire sauce
⅛ teaspoon pepper
6 Kaiser rolls *or* hamburger buns, split and toasted

1. In 10-inch skillet over medium-high heat, cook beef until browned,
   stirring to separate meat. Spoon off fat.

2. Stir in soup, water, Worcestershire and pepper. Heat through, stirring
   occasionally. Serve on rolls.

Makes about 3 cups or 6 servings	Prep Time: 5 minutes Cook Time: 10 minutes

Souper Joes: Prepare Shortcut Sloppy Joes as directed above, *except*
substitute 1 pound *bulk pork sausage* for the ground beef. In step 1, add
½ cup chopped *green pepper* with the sausage. In step 2, omit water,
Worcestershire and pepper. Serve on 4 *hard rolls* (each about 7 inches
long), split and toasted. Makes 4 servings.

Fabulous Casseroles and Bakes

CHICKEN–CHEESE ENCHILADAS

A zesty mixture of salsa, cooked chicken and green chilies fill the flour tortillas. This casserole can also be made with Cheddar Cheese Soup.

1 can (11 ounces) CAMPBELL'S condensed Nacho Cheese Soup
½ cup milk
2 cups diced cooked chicken
½ cup salsa
1 can (4 ounces) chopped green chilies
1 teaspoon chili powder
8 flour tortillas (8 inches *each*)

1. In small bowl, combine soup and milk; set aside.

2. In medium bowl, combine chicken, salsa, chilies, chili powder and *2 tablespoons* of soup mixture.

3. To make enchiladas, along one side of each tortilla, spread about ⅓ cup of chicken mixture. Roll up each tortilla, jelly-roll fashion; place seam-side down in greased 3-quart oblong baking dish.

4. Spread remaining soup mixture over enchiladas. Cover with foil. Bake at 375°F. for 35 minutes or until hot and bubbling.

Makes 4 servings	Prep Time: 15 minutes Cook Time: 35 minutes

Tip Prepare Chicken-Cheese Enchiladas as directed above. Top with any of the following: *sour cream,* sliced pitted *ripe olives, salsa, guacamole,* sliced *green onions* and/or shredded *Cheddar cheese* before serving. *(Pictured)*

Chicken-Cheese Enchiladas

ZESTY CHICKEN BAKE

Use a combination of chicken breasts and legs to make this saucy main dish.

4 chicken breast halves *or* legs (about 2 pounds)
1 can (11⅛ ounces) CAMPBELL'S condensed Italian Tomato Soup
1 tablespoon packed brown sugar
1 tablespoon water
1 tablespoon vinegar
1 tablespoon Worcestershire sauce
  Hot cooked corkscrew macaroni
  Fresh rosemary sprig for garnish

1. Remove skin from chicken. In 2-quart oblong baking dish, arrange chicken. Cover with foil. Bake at 375°F. for 30 minutes.

2. Meanwhile, in small bowl, combine soup, brown sugar, water, vinegar and Worcestershire; set aside.

3. Spoon soup mixture over chicken. Bake, uncovered, 30 minutes more or until chicken is no longer pink and juices run clear.

4. To serve, arrange chicken over macaroni. Stir sauce and spoon over chicken. Garnish with rosemary, if desired.

Makes 4 servings	Prep Time: 5 minutes Cook Time: 1 hour

Zesty Pork Chop Bake: Prepare Zesty Chicken Bake as directed above, *except*, substitute 6 *pork loin chops*, each cut 1-inch thick (about 2½ pounds) for the chicken. Arrange chops in 3-quart oblong baking dish. Bake, uncovered, at 400°F. for 20 minutes or until chops begin to brown. Spoon off fat. In step 2, stir ¼ to ½ teaspoon *hot pepper sauce* into soup mixture. Spoon soup mixture over chops. Bake 15 minutes more or until chops are no longer pink. Serve as directed in step 4. Makes 6 servings.

CHICKEN POT PIE

Ready-to-use refrigerated biscuits are the topper in this hearty main-dish pie.

1 can (10¾ ounces) CAMPBELL'S condensed Cream of Broccoli Soup
1 can (10¾ ounces) CAMPBELL'S condensed Creamy Chicken Mushroom Soup
1 cup milk
¼ teaspoon dried thyme leaves, crushed
¼ teaspoon pepper
4 cups cooked cut-up vegetables (broccoli, cauliflower, carrots and potatoes)
2 cups cubed cooked chicken *or* turkey
1 package (7½ ounces) refrigerated biscuits (10)

1. In 3-quart oblong baking dish, combine soups, milk, thyme and pepper. Stir in vegetables and chicken.

2. Bake at 400°F. for 15 minutes or until mixture begins to bubble. Stir. Meanwhile, cut each biscuit into quarters, cutting almost but not all the way through the bottom.

3. Remove dish from oven; stir. Arrange biscuits over hot chicken mixture. Bake 15 minutes more or until biscuits are golden brown.

Makes about 6½ cups or 5 servings	Prep Time: 15 minutes Cook Time: 30 minutes

Tip Prepare Chicken Pot Pie as directed above, *except* substitute *half-and-half* for the milk. In step 2, brush uncooked biscuits with 1 tablespoon *margarine or butter*, melted, and sprinkle 1 teaspoon *poppy seeds* over the biscuits.

TURKEY TETRAZZINI

Here's a great idea for your next potluck party: Use a thermal container, ice chest or sturdy insulated bag to keep this casserole hot while transporting.

1 can (10¾ ounces) **CAMPBELL'S condensed Cream of Mushroom Soup**
½ **cup milk**
¼ **cup grated Parmesan cheese**
¼ **cup finely chopped onion**
¼ **cup sour cream**
1½ **cups cubed cooked turkey** *or* **chicken**
1 **small zucchini, cut in half lengthwise and thinly sliced (about 1 cup)**
1½ **cups cooked spaghetti (3 ounces dry)**

1. In large bowl, combine soup, milk, Parmesan cheese, onion and sour cream. Stir in turkey and zucchini. Add spaghetti; toss gently to coat. Spoon into 1½-quart baking dish or casserole.

2. Bake at 375°F. for 30 minutes or until hot and bubbling. Serve with additional Parmesan cheese, if desired.

Makes about 4 cups or 4 servings	Prep Time: 20 minutes Cook Time: 30 minutes

Tip   Prepare Turkey Tetrazzini as directed above. Garnish with *carrot curl, fresh thyme sprigs, Parmesan cheese* and toasted *sliced almonds*. *(Pictured)*

Turkey Tetrazzini

MEDITERRANEAN CHICKEN

Bulgur is wheat kernels that have been steamed, dried and crushed. It has a tender, chewy texture and is delicious in meat or vegetable dishes.

1½ cups bulgur wheat *or* regular long-grain rice, uncooked
  1 can (about 16 ounces) stewed tomatoes, cut up
  1 can (10½ ounces) CAMPBELL'S condensed Chicken Broth
½ soup can water
¼ cup chopped fresh parsley
¼ cup sliced pitted ripe olives
  1 tablespoon lemon juice
½ teaspoon pepper
  6 skinless, boneless chicken breast halves (about 1½ pounds)
½ teaspoon garlic salt
  Paprika

1. In 3-quart oblong baking dish, combine bulgur wheat, tomatoes, broth, water, parsley, olives, lemon juice and pepper.

2. Arrange chicken on bulgur mixture; press each chicken breast into bulgur mixture, covering halfway. Sprinkle garlic salt and paprika over chicken. Cover with foil.

3. Bake at 375°F. for 30 minutes. Uncover; bake 10 minutes more or until chicken is no longer pink. Garnish with additional parsley and olives, if desired.

Makes 6 servings	Prep Time: 10 minutes Cook Time: 40 minutes

Tip Prepare Mediterranean Chicken as directed above, *except* substitute 2 tablespoons chopped *fresh mint* for the parsley. Garnish with additional olives and *fresh mint sprig*, if desired. *(Pictured)*

Mediterranean Chicken

MEXICAN TUNA–MACARONI BAKE

1 can (10¾ ounces) CAMPBELL'S condensed Golden Corn Soup
¾ cup milk
1 cup shredded Monterey Jack cheese (4 ounces)
½ cup salsa
3½ cups cooked corkscrew macaroni (about 3 cups dry)
1 can (about 7 ounces) tuna, drained and broken into chunks
1 small tomato, chopped
1 cup broken tortilla chips
Fresh cilantro for garnish

1. In medium bowl, combine soup and milk. Stir in Monterey Jack cheese and salsa. Add macaroni and tuna; toss gently to coat. Spoon into 2-quart oblong baking dish.

2. Bake at 375°F. for 30 minutes or until hot and bubbling. Top with tomato. Arrange tortilla chips around edge of casserole. Garnish with cilantro, if desired.

Makes about 5 cups or 5 servings	Prep Time: 25 minutes Cook Time: 30 minutes

Tip   Prepare Mexican Tuna-Macaroni Bake as directed above, *except* make your own salsa. To prepare Fresh Salsa, in small bowl, combine 1 medium *tomato*, seeded and chopped, ¼ cup chopped *green onions*, 1 tablespoon *lime juice*, 2 teaspoons chopped *fresh cilantro*, ½ to 1 teaspoon finely chopped *jalapeño pepper* and ¼ teaspoon *garlic salt*. In step 1, use ½ cup fresh salsa. In step 2, omit chopped tomato and top with remaining fresh salsa. Makes about 1¼ cups salsa.

SHORTCUT TUNA LASAGNA

Mafalda is a small, flat noodle that resembles ripple-edged lasagna. You can substitute 4 cups cooked rigatoni or corkscrew macaroni for the mafalda.

1 can (10¾ ounces) CAMPBELL'S condensed Cream of Mushroom Soup
½ cup milk
1 cup shredded Monterey Jack cheese (4 ounces)
½ cup spaghetti sauce
⅓ cup grated Parmesan cheese
3½ cups cooked mafalda (mini lasagna) pasta (about 3 cups dry)
1 can (about 7 ounces) tuna, drained and broken into chunks
½ cup seasoned croutons

1. In medium bowl, combine soup and milk. Stir in Monterey Jack cheese, spaghetti sauce and Parmesan cheese. Add pasta and tuna; toss gently to coat. Spoon into 2-quart oblong baking dish.

2. Bake at 375°F. for 25 minutes.

3. Top with croutons. Bake 5 minutes more or until hot and bubbling.

Makes about 5 cups or 5 servings	Prep Time: 25 minutes Cook Time: 30 minutes

Salmon Pasta Bake: Prepare Shortcut Tuna Lasagna as directed above, *except* substitute 1 can (about 7 ounces) *salmon*, drained and broken into chunks, for the tuna. In step 3, arrange 1 large *plum tomato*, sliced, and croutons over the pasta mixture. Continue baking as directed. Garnish with *fresh basil*, if desired. *(Pictured)*

Salmon Pasta Bake

THREE–CHEESE PASTA BAKE

Mostaccioli are large, 2-inch-long macaroni tubes, with smooth or ridged surfaces, that are cut on a diagonal.

1 can (11 ounces) CAMPBELL'S condensed Cheddar Cheese Soup
¾ cup milk
¼ teaspoon pepper
1 cup shredded mozzarella cheese (4 ounces)
6 cups cooked mostaccioli *or* ziti (about 3 cups dry)
2 tablespoons grated Parmesan cheese
2 tablespoons dry bread crumbs
1 tablespoon margarine *or* butter, melted
Fresh parsley sprig *and* tomato slices for garnish

1. In large bowl, combine soup, milk and pepper. Stir in mozzarella cheese. Add mostaccioli; toss gently to coat. Spoon into 2-quart oblong baking dish.

2. Sprinkle Parmesan cheese over pasta mixture. In small bowl, combine bread crumbs and margarine; sprinkle crumb mixture in rows over cheese.

3. Bake at 375°F. for 35 minutes or until hot and bubbling. Garnish with parsley and tomato, if desired.

Makes about 6 cups or 6 servings	Prep Time: 25 minutes Cook Time: 35 minutes

Tip Prepare Three-Cheese Pasta Bake as directed above, *except* in step 1, reduce shredded mozzarella cheese to ¾ cup (3 ounces) and add ½ cup shredded *smoked Edam or smoked Gouda cheese* (2 ounces).

GOLDEN CORN STUFFING BAKE

1 can (10¾ ounces) CAMPBELL'S condensed Golden Corn Soup
1½ cups corn bread stuffing
¼ cup thinly sliced celery
¼ cup finely chopped onion
4 skinless, boneless chicken breast halves (about 1 pound)
1 tablespoon packed brown sugar
1 tablespoon margarine *or* butter, melted
1 teaspoon spicy brown mustard
Fresh sage leaves for garnish

1. In medium bowl, combine soup, stuffing, celery and onion. Spoon stuffing mixture into greased 9-inch pie plate. Arrange chicken over stuffing mixture; press each chicken breast lightly into stuffing mixture.

2. In small bowl, combine sugar, margarine and mustard. Add generous dash *paprika*, if desired. Spread mixture evenly over chicken.

3. Bake at 400°F. for 25 minutes or until chicken is no longer pink. Garnish with sage, if desired. Stir stuffing before serving.

Makes about 2 cups stuffing and 4 servings	Prep Time: 10 minutes Cook Time: 25 minutes

Corn and Pork Stuffing Bake: Prepare Golden Corn Stuffing Bake as directed above, *except* substitute 4 boneless *pork chops*, each cut ¾ inch thick (about 1 pound), for the chicken. In step 1, add ⅓ cup *raisins* or chopped *mixed dried fruits* with the soup. In step 2, omit margarine. In step 3, bake 30 minutes or until chops are no longer pink. Serve as directed in step 3.

HARVEST PORK ROAST

  2 tablespoons vegetable oil
3½- to 4-pound boneless pork shoulder roast, netted or tied
     (Boston butt)
  1 can (10¾ ounces) CAMPBELL'S condensed Cream of Mushroom
     Soup
  1 pouch CAMPBELL'S Dry Onion Quality Soup and Recipe Mix
1¼ cups water
  1 teaspoon dried thyme leaves, crushed
  1 bay leaf
  8 medium potatoes, quartered
  8 medium carrots, cut into 2-inch pieces
  2 tablespoons all-purpose flour

1. In oven-safe 5-quart Dutch oven over medium-high heat, in hot oil, cook roast until browned on all sides. Remove; set aside. Spoon off fat.

2. In same Dutch oven, combine soups, *1 cup* of water, thyme and bay leaf. Heat to boiling, stirring occasionally. Return roast to Dutch oven. Cover; bake at 350°F. for 45 minutes.

3. Turn roast. Add potatoes and carrots. Cover; bake 1 hour 45 minutes more or until vegetables are fork-tender and roast is no longer pink (170°F. internal temperature).

4. Transfer roast and vegetables to platter. Remove netting or string from roast. In small bowl, stir together flour and remaining ¼ cup water until smooth. In Dutch oven over medium heat, heat soup mixture to boiling. Gradually stir in flour mixture. Cook until mixture boils and thickens, stirring constantly. Remove bay leaf. Serve gravy with roast.

Makes about 3 cups gravy and 8 servings	Prep Time: 5 minutes Cook Time: 2 hours 45 minutes

Tip   Prepare Harvest Pork Roast as directed above, *except* substitute 1 tablespoon *fresh thyme leaves* for the dried thyme leaves, 1½ pounds *small red potatoes* (about 15) for the potatoes and ¾ pound *baby patty pan squash* (about 12) for the carrots. In step 3, add red potatoes as directed. Bake 1 hour 20 minutes, then add squash. Continue baking as directed. Garnish with *fresh thyme sprig,* if desired. *(Pictured)*

Harvest Pork Roast

SAVORY MEAT LOAF AND VEGETABLES

2 cans (10¾ ounces *each*) CAMPBELL'S condensed Golden
   Mushroom Soup
1½ pounds ground beef
 ½ cup dry bread crumbs
 ¼ cup finely chopped onion
 1 tablespoon Worcestershire sauce
 ⅛ teaspoon pepper
 1 egg, beaten
 6 medium potatoes, quartered
 6 medium carrots, cut into 2-inch pieces
 ¾ cup water
   Fresh rosemary sprigs *and* fluted fresh mushrooms for garnish

1. In large bowl, mix thoroughly ½ *cup* of soup, beef, bread crumbs, onion, Worcestershire, pepper and egg. In 3-quart oblong baking dish, *firmly* shape meat into 8-by 4-inch loaf. Arrange potatoes and carrots around meat loaf.

2. Bake at 375°F. for 45 minutes. Spoon off fat.

3. Meanwhile, in small bowl, combine remaining soup and water. Pour soup mixture over vegetables and meat loaf. Bake 30 minutes more or until vegetables are fork-tender and meat loaf is no longer pink (160°F. internal temperature).

4. To serve, arrange meat loaf with vegetables on platter. Spoon some sauce over meat loaf; pass remaining sauce. Garnish with rosemary and mushrooms, if desired.

Makes 6 servings	Prep Time: 15 minutes
	Cook Time: 1 hour 15 minutes

Tip Prepare Savory Meat Loaf and Vegetables as directed above, *except* substitute ground meat loaf mix (½ pound each ground *beef, pork and veal*) for the ground beef. In step 3, reduce water to ½ *cup* and add ¼ cup *Burgundy or other dry red wine*. Bake until meat loaf is no longer pink (170°F. internal temperature).

Savory Meat Loaf and Vegetables

Fabulous Soups and Stews

SEAFOOD CHOWDER

1 tablespoon vegetable oil
1 cup chopped onion
1 clove garlic, minced
¼ teaspoon dried dill weed, crushed
1 can (10¾ ounces) CAMPBELL'S condensed Cream of Celery Soup
1 can (10¾ ounces) CAMPBELL'S condensed Cream of Potato Soup
1½ soup cans milk
½ pound medium shrimp, shelled and deveined
½ pound firm white fish fillets, cut into 2-inch pieces
 Chopped fresh parsley for garnish

1. In 3-quart saucepan over medium heat, in hot oil, cook onion, garlic and dill until onion is tender, stirring occasionally.

2. Stir in soups and milk. Heat to boiling, stirring often. Cook 8 minutes. Reduce heat to low.

3. Add shrimp and fish. Cook 5 minutes more or until shrimp turn pink and opaque and fish flakes easily when tested with fork, stirring occasionally.

4. To serve, ladle soup into bowls. Garnish with parsley, if desired.

Makes about 6½ cups or 4 main-dish servings	Prep Time: 15 minutes Cook Time: 20 minutes

Tip Prepare Seafood Chowder as directed above, *except* in step 1, substitute 2 teaspoons chopped *fresh dill* for the dried dill weed. In step 2, add 2 tablespoons *Chablis or other dry white wine.* Garnish with *fresh dill sprigs,* if desired. *(Pictured)*

Seafood Chowder

SPICY VEGETABLE CHILI

Chick peas, black beans, zucchini and carrots are simmered in flavorful Tomato Soup and Creamy Onion Soup for this main-dish soup.

1 can (10¾ ounces) CAMPBELL'S condensed Tomato Soup
1 can (10¾ ounces) CAMPBELL'S condensed Creamy Onion Soup
2 soup cans water
1 can (about 16 ounces) chick peas (garbanzo beans),
    rinsed and drained
1 can (about 16 ounces) black beans, rinsed and drained
2 medium zucchini, coarsely chopped (about 2 cups)
2 medium carrots, coarsely chopped (about 1 cup)
1 tablespoon chili powder
½ teaspoon dried thyme leaves, crushed
⅛ teaspoon pepper

1. In 4-quart saucepan, combine soups and water. Stir in chick peas, black beans, zucchini, carrots, chili powder, thyme and pepper.

2. Over medium heat, heat to boiling. Reduce heat to low. Cook 40 minutes, stirring occasionally.

3. To serve, ladle chili into bowls.

Makes about 8 cups or 6 main-dish servings	Prep Time: 10 minutes Cook Time: 50 minutes

Tip   Prepare Spicy Vegetable Chili as directed above. Serve with *sour cream*, shredded *Cheddar cheese* and chopped *green pepper*. Garnish with *fresh jalapeño pepper*, if desired. *(Pictured)*

Spicy Vegetable Chili

POTATO–CORN CHOWDER

For crisp-cooked bacon in a hurry, microwave it. One slice of bacon cooks in about one minute on high power.

1 tablespoon margarine *or* butter
½ cup chopped celery
1 medium onion, chopped
1½ cups diced peeled potatoes
1 cup water
⅛ teaspoon pepper
1 bay leaf
1 can (10¾ ounces) CAMPBELL'S condensed Golden Corn Soup
1 cup milk
4 slices bacon, cooked and crumbled, for garnish
Fresh bay leaf for garnish

1. In 3-quart saucepan over medium heat, in hot margarine, cook celery and onion 5 minutes or until tender, stirring occasionally.

2. Add potatoes, water, pepper and bay leaf. Heat to boiling. Reduce heat to low. Cover; cook 15 minutes or until potatoes are tender, stirring occasionally.

3. Gradually stir in soup and milk. Cook, uncovered, 5 minutes, stirring occasionally. Remove bay leaf.

4. To serve, ladle soup into bowls. Garnish with bacon and fresh bay leaf, if desired.

Makes about 4½ cups or 4 side-dish servings	Prep Time: 15 minutes Cook Time: 30 minutes

Seafood-Corn Chowder: Prepare Potato-Corn Chowder as directed above, *except* reduce milk to ½ cup and add ½ cup *half-and-half*. In step 3, add 1 cup cut-up cooked *fish or seafood* (clams, oysters, shrimp, salmon or cod) with the soup.

Potato-Corn Chowder

PORK STEW MEXICANO

Garlic, cumin and oregano give this savory stew its Mexican taste.

1 tablespoon vegetable oil
1½ pounds boneless pork shoulder, cut into ¾-inch pieces
2 cloves garlic, minced
1 teaspoon ground cumin
1 teaspoon dried oregano leaves, crushed
1 can (about 28 ounces) tomatoes, undrained and cut up
1 can (10¾ ounces) CAMPBELL'S condensed Creamy Onion Soup
1 can (10¾ ounces) CAMPBELL'S condensed Golden Corn Soup
2 medium zucchini, cut in half lengthwise and thinly sliced
     (about 3 cups)
1 tablespoon chopped fresh parsley
  Fresh parsley sprig for garnish

1. In 5-quart Dutch oven over medium-high heat, in hot oil, cook *half* of pork until browned, stirring often. Remove; set aside. Repeat with remaining pork. Return pork to Dutch oven. Add garlic, cumin and oregano. Cook 2 minutes, stirring occasionally.

2. Stir in *undrained* tomatoes and soups. Heat to boiling, stirring occasionally. Reduce heat to low. Cover; cook 40 minutes, stirring occasionally.

3. Stir in zucchini. Heat to boiling. Reduce heat to low. Cover; cook 15 minutes or until pork and zucchini are fork-tender. Stir in chopped parsley. Garnish with parsley sprig, if desired.

4. To serve, ladle stew into bowls.

Makes about 8 cups or 6 main-dish servings	Prep Time: 15 minutes Cook Time: 1 hour 15 minutes

Tip Prepare Pork Stew Mexicano as directed above. Serve topped with *sour cream* and *sliced avocado.*

Pork Stew Mexicano

QUICK CASSOULET

*In less than 1 hour you can make this shortcut version
of the classic French dish.*

1 can (10¾ ounces) CAMPBELL'S condensed Creamy Onion Soup
1 can (10¾ ounces) CAMPBELL'S condensed Tomato Soup
1 cup water
1 can (about 16 ounces) small white beans, rinsed and drained
¾ pound kielbasa, cut into ½-inch slices
 4 small potatoes (12 ounces), peeled and quartered
 3 medium carrots, cut into ½-inch pieces (1 cup)
½ teaspoon dried thyme leaves, crushed
⅛ teaspoon pepper
 1 bay leaf
   Chopped fresh parsley for garnish

1. In 4- or 5-quart Dutch oven, combine soups and water. Stir in beans, kielbasa, potatoes, carrots, thyme, pepper and bay leaf. Over medium heat, heat to boiling, stirring occasionally.

2. Reduce heat to low. Cover; cook 25 minutes or until vegetables are tender, stirring occasionally. Remove bay leaf. Garnish with parsley, if desired.

3. To serve, ladle cassoulet into bowls.

Makes about 8 cups or 5 main-dish servings	Prep Time: 10 minutes Cook Time: 35 minutes

Tip Prepare Quick Cassoulet as directed above, *except* reduce water to ¾ cup and add ¼ cup *Chablis or other dry white wine.* Substitute 1½ teaspoons chopped *fresh thyme leaves* for the dried thyme leaves. In step 2, add fresh thyme leaves to the soup mixture during the last 10 minutes of cooking. Garnish with *fresh thyme leaves,* if desired. *(Pictured)*

Quick Cassoulet

VEAL RAGOUT

2 tablespoons olive *or* vegetable oil
1½ pounds veal for stew, cut into 1-inch pieces
1 can (10¾ ounces) CAMPBELL'S condensed Creamy Chicken
    Mushroom Soup
½ cup water
½ cup Chablis *or* other dry white wine
1 teaspoon lemon juice
¼ teaspoon pepper
1 clove garlic, minced
1½ cups diagonally sliced carrots
2 tablespoons chopped fresh parsley
   Hot cooked rice (optional)

1. In 5-quart Dutch oven over medium-high heat, in hot oil, cook *half* of veal until lightly browned, stirring often. Remove; set aside. Repeat with remaining veal.

2. In same Dutch oven combine soup, water, wine, lemon juice, pepper and garlic. Return veal to Dutch oven. Add carrots. Heat to boiling. Reduce heat to low. Cover; cook 45 minutes, stirring occasionally.

3. Uncover; cook 15 minutes more or until soup mixture is thickened and veal is fork-tender, stirring occasionally.

4. Stir in *1 tablespoon* parsley. Sprinkle with remaining parsley. Serve with rice, if desired.

Makes about 4 cups or 4 main-dish servings	Prep Time: 15 minutes Cook Time: 1 hour 15 minutes

Tip Prepare Veal Ragout as directed above, *except* in step 2, add 1½ teaspoons chopped *fresh rosemary leaves* or ½ teaspoon *dried rosemary leaves*, crushed, with the soup. In step 3, add 1 cup *fresh small mushrooms*, each cut in half. Garnish with *fresh rosemary sprig*, if desired. *(Pictured)*

Veal Ragout

CHILI BEEF SOUP

½ **pound ground beef**
¾ **cup chopped onion**
 1 **clove garlic, minced**
 1 **can (about 15 ounces) kidney beans, rinsed and drained**
 1 **can (about 15 ounces) tomatoes, undrained and cut up**
 1 **can (10¾ ounces) CAMPBELL'S condensed Beefy Mushroom Soup**
½ **cup water**
 2 **teaspoons chili powder**
¼ **teaspoon ground cumin**
⅛ **teaspoon pepper**
 1 **bay leaf**

1. In 4-quart saucepan over medium-high heat, cook beef, onion and garlic until beef is browned and onion is tender, stirring to separate meat. Spoon off fat.

2. Stir in beans, *undrained* tomatoes, soup, water, chili powder, cumin, pepper and bay leaf. Heat to boiling. Reduce heat to low. Cover; cook 15 minutes to blend flavors, stirring occasionally. Remove bay leaf.

3. To serve, ladle soup into bowls.

Makes about 5 cups or 4 main-dish servings	Prep Time: 10 minutes Cook Time: 25 minutes

Tip Prepare Chili Beef Soup as directed above. Serve topped with *sour cream*, shredded *Cheddar cheese*, chopped *green pepper* and sliced, pitted *ripe olives. (Pictured)*

Chili Beef Soup

OVEN BEEF SOUP

You can substitute 1½ teaspoons chopped fresh thyme leaves for the dried thyme leaves in this recipe.

  2 tablespoons vegetable oil
1½ pounds beef for stew, cut into 1-inch pieces
  1 can (10¾ ounces) CAMPBELL'S condensed Beefy Mushroom Soup
  1 can (10¾ ounces) CAMPBELL'S condensed Golden Mushroom Soup
  1 cup water
  ½ teaspoon dried thyme leaves, crushed
  ½ teaspoon pepper
  1 bay leaf
  3 cups cubed peeled potatoes
  1 cup carrots cut in chunks
  1 cup celery cut in chunks
     Fresh thyme sprigs for garnish

1. In 5-quart oven-safe Dutch oven over medium-high heat, in hot oil, cook *half* of beef until browned, stirring often. Remove; set aside. Repeat with remaining beef. Spoon off fat.

2. In same Dutch oven, combine soups, water, thyme, pepper and bay leaf. Return beef to Dutch oven. Add potatoes, carrots and celery. Heat to boiling. Cover; remove from heat.

3. Bake at 350°F. for 2 hours. Remove bay leaf.

4. To serve, ladle soup into bowls. Garnish with thyme sprigs, if desired.

Makes about 7½ cups or 6 main-dish servings	Prep Time: 20 minutes Cook Time: 2 hours 20 minutes

Tip Prepare Oven Beef Soup as directed above, *except* reduce water to ½ cup, reduce potatoes to 2 cups and omit carrot chunks. In step 2, add ½ cup *dry white vermouth* with the soup. Add 1 cup fresh *baby carrots* and ½ pound fresh *small white onions*, peeled, leaving a little of root ends to help the onions hold their shape during cooking, with the browned beef.

Fabulous Six-Ingredient Sides

GOLDEN CORN AND BROCCOLI

Cherry tomatoes and chopped fresh basil leaves are used to make Tomato, Corn and Broccoli, as shown here and on the front cover.

1 bunch (about 1½ pounds) fresh broccoli, cut up *or* 1 package (20 ounces) frozen broccoli cuts
1 cup water
1 can (10¾ ounces) CAMPBELL'S condensed Golden Corn Soup
½ cup shredded Cheddar cheese (2 ounces)
¼ cup milk
Generous dash pepper

1. In 3-quart saucepan, combine broccoli and water. Over high heat, heat to boiling. Reduce heat to low. Cover; cook 8 minutes or until broccoli is tender-crisp, stirring occasionally. Drain in colander.

2. In same saucepan, combine soup, Cheddar cheese, milk and pepper. Return broccoli to saucepan. Over medium heat, heat through, stirring occasionally.

Makes about 5 cups or 8 servings	Prep Time: 10 minutes Cook Time: 15 minutes

Tomato, Corn and Broccoli: Prepare Golden Corn and Broccoli as directed above, *except* in step 2, add 1 tablespoon chopped *fresh basil leaves* with the soup. Add 1 cup quartered *cherry tomatoes* before serving. *(Pictured)*

Tomato, Corn and Broccoli

CHEDDAR–POTATO BAKE

*Tastes just as delicious when made with Broccoli Cheese Soup
or Golden Corn Soup.*

1 can (11 ounces) CAMPBELL'S condensed Cheddar Cheese Soup
⅓ cup sour cream *or* plain yogurt
2 tablespoons chopped green onion
   Generous dash pepper
3 cups stiff, seasoned mashed potatoes

1. In 1½-quart casserole, combine soup, sour cream, onion and pepper. Stir in potatoes until blended.

2. Bake at 350°F. for 30 minutes or until hot and bubbling. Garnish with shredded *Cheddar cheese* and sliced *green onion,* if desired.

Makes about 4½ cups or 8 servings	Prep Time: 10 minutes Cook Time: 30 minutes

Crumb-Topped Potato Bake: Prepare Cheddar-Potato Bake as directed above. In small bowl, combine 2 tablespoons *dry bread crumbs,* 1 tablespoon *margarine or butter,* melted, and ¼ teaspoon *paprika.* In step 2, sprinkle bread crumb mixture over potato mixture before baking.

Tip This recipe can be prepared on top of the range. In 2-quart saucepan, combine soup, sour cream, onion and pepper. Stir in potatoes until blended. Over low heat, heat through, stirring occasionally.

SHORTCUT RISOTTO

For a change of pace, you can make any one of these easy risottos with a can of condensed Beef Broth.

1 tablespoon margarine *or* butter
1 cup regular long-grain rice, uncooked
½ cup chopped onion
1 can (10½ ounces) CAMPBELL'S condensed Chicken Broth
1 soup can water
3 tablespoons grated Parmesan cheese

1. In 2-quart saucepan over medium-high heat, in hot margarine, cook rice and onion 5 minutes or until rice is browned and onion is tender, stirring constantly.

2. Slowly stir in broth and water. Heat to boiling. Reduce heat to low. Cover; cook 20 minutes or until rice is tender and liquid is absorbed.

3. Remove from heat. Stir in Parmesan cheese. Garnish with *green onion curls* and *lemon wedges,* if desired.

Makes about 3 cups or 6 servings	Prep Time: 5 minutes Cook Time: 30 minutes

Risotto with Peas: Prepare Shortcut Risotto as directed above, *except* in step 1, cook ¼ cup finely chopped *prosciutto* with the rice. In step 2, add 1 cup *frozen peas* during last 5 minutes of cooking. Garnish with quartered *lemon slices,* if desired. Makes about 4 cups.

Risotto Verde: Prepare Shortcut Risotto as directed above, *except* substitute ½ cup sliced *green onions* for the chopped onion. In step 1, cook ¼ cup chopped *celery* with the green onions. In step 2, add 2 cups chopped *fresh spinach* with the broth. Garnish with *lemon peel curls,* if desired. Makes about 4 cups.

Clockwise from top: Risotto with Peas, Risotto Verde and Shortcut Risotto

CORN VEGETABLE MEDLEY

Next time, make this easy vegetable combo with Cream of Mushroom Soup or Cream of Celery Soup.

    1 can (10¾ ounces) CAMPBELL'S condensed Golden Corn Soup
    ½ cup milk
    2 cups broccoli flowerets
    1 cup sliced carrots
    1 cup cauliflowerets
    ½ cup shredded Cheddar cheese (2 ounces) (optional)

1. In 2-quart saucepan over medium heat, heat soup and milk to boiling. Stir in broccoli, carrots and cauliflowerets.

2. Return to boiling. Reduce heat to low. Cover; cook 20 minutes or until vegetables are tender, stirring occasionally. Stir in Cheddar cheese. Heat through until cheese melts. Garnish with *fresh chives*, if desired.

Makes about 3½ cups or 6 servings	Prep Time: 10 minutes Cook Time: 25 minutes

Peppery Vegetable Medley: Prepare Corn Vegetable Medley as directed above, *except* in step 1, cook ⅓ cup diced *sweet red pepper* with the broccoli. In step 2, add 1 tablespoon chopped *fresh cilantro* and ½ to 1 teaspoon *Louisiana-style hot sauce* with the Cheddar cheese.

CHEDDAR–BROCCOLI NOODLES

4 cups water
2 packages (3 ounces *each*) **CAMPBELL'S** *or* **RAMEN PRIDE**
    Chicken Flavor Ramen Noodle Soup
1½ cups broccoli flowerets
1 can (11 ounces) CAMPBELL'S condensed Cheddar Cheese Soup
¼ cup sour cream *or* **plain yogurt**
⅛ teaspoon pepper

1. In 3-quart saucepan over high heat, heat water to boiling. Add noodles
   and broccoli. Return to boiling. Reduce heat to low. Cover; cook
   5 minutes or until noodles and broccoli are tender, stirring occasionally
   to separate noodles.

2. Stir in *one* seasoning packet; drain off most of liquid. (Reserve
   remaining seasoning packet for another use.)

3. Stir in cheese soup, sour cream and pepper. Heat through, stirring
   occasionally. Garnish with matchstick-thin strips *sweet red pepper*, if
   desired.

Makes about 4 cups or 6 servings	Prep Time: 10 minutes Cook Time: 15 minutes

Tip Prepare Cheddar-Broccoli Noodles as directed above. Sprinkle
with grated *fresh Parmesan cheese* before serving.

QUICK LEMON–BROCCOLI RICE

This fast-to-fix dish can be made with either quick-cooking white or brown rice.

1 can (10½ ounces) CAMPBELL'S condensed Chicken Broth
1 cup small broccoli flowerets
⅓ cup shredded carrot
1¼ cups quick-cooking rice, uncooked
2 teaspoons lemon juice
  Generous dash pepper

1. In 2-quart saucepan over high heat, heat broth to boiling. Add broccoli and carrot. Return to boiling. Reduce heat to low. Cover; cook 5 minutes or until vegetables are tender.

2. Stir in rice, lemon juice and pepper. Remove from heat. Cover; let stand 5 minutes or until liquid is absorbed. Fluff rice with fork before serving. Garnish with *lemon slices* and *fresh tarragon sprig,* if desired.

Makes about 3 cups or 4 servings	Prep Time: 10 minutes Cook Time: 15 minutes

Brown Rice with Broccoli: Prepare Quick Lemon-Broccoli Rice as directed above, *except* substitute *1 cup quick-cooking brown rice,* uncooked, for the quick-cooking rice. In step 1, cook rice with vegetables. In step 2, stir in 2 teaspoons chopped *fresh basil leaves or parsley* just before serving. Makes 2½ to 3 cups.

Quick Lemon-Broccoli Rice

TOMATO–BASIL PASTA SAUCE

You can also serve this pasta sauce over hot cooked linguini, spaghetti or multi-colored fusilli.

1 can (10¾ ounces) **CAMPBELL'S** condensed Broccoli Cheese Soup
¾ cup half-and-half *or* milk
3 fresh plum tomatoes, coarsely chopped (about 1 cup) *or* 4 canned
    plum tomatoes, drained and coarsely chopped (about ¾ cup)
¼ cup grated Parmesan cheese
1 tablespoon chopped fresh basil leaves *or* 1 teaspoon dried basil
    leaves, crushed
3 cups hot cooked fettuccine (6 ounces dry)

1. In 2-quart saucepan, stir soup, half-and-half, chopped tomatoes, Parmesan cheese and basil. Over medium heat, heat to boiling. Reduce heat to low; cook 5 minutes, stirring occasionally.

2. Pour over fettuccine; toss gently to coat. Garnish with sliced *fresh plum tomato* and *fresh basil sprig,* if desired.

Makes about 4 cups or 4 servings	Prep Time: 20 minutes Cook Time: 10 minutes

Tip   Prepare Tomato-Basil Pasta Sauce as directed above. Sprinkle with toasted *pine nuts* before serving. *(Pictured)*

Tomato-Basil Pasta Sauce

CLASSIC GREEN BEAN BAKE

*Pictured here, Corn and Bean Amandine is made with
Campbell's Golden Corn Soup.*

1 can (10¾ ounces) CAMPBELL'S condensed Cream of Mushroom
    Soup
½ cup milk
1 teaspoon soy sauce
    Generous dash pepper
2 packages (9 ounces *each*) frozen cut green beans, cooked and
    drained (4 cups)
1 can (2.8 ounces) French fried onions

1. In 1½-quart casserole, combine soup, milk, soy sauce and pepper. Stir
   in beans and ½ *can* of onions.

2. Bake at 350°F. for 25 minutes or until hot and bubbling.

3. Stir bean mixture. Top with remaining onions. Bake 5 minutes more or
   until hot and bubbling.

Makes about 4½ cups or 6 servings	Prep Time: 10 minutes Cook Time: 30 minutes

Corn and Bean Amandine: Prepare Classic Green Bean Bake as directed
above, *except* substitute 1 can (10¾ ounces) CAMPBELL'S condensed
Golden Corn Soup for the Cream of Mushroom Soup. In step 3, stir in
¼ cup toasted *slivered or sliced almonds*. Top with remaining onions.
Continue baking as directed. *(Pictured)*

Tip Substitute 1½ pounds fresh green beans, cut in 1-inch pieces,
cooked and drained, or 2 cans (about 16 ounces *each*) cut green beans,
drained, for the frozen cut green beans.

Corn and Bean Amandine

HANDY KITCHEN TIPS

Buying Canned Salmon
● Before you buy canned salmon, consider how you plan to prepare it. When the appearance is important in a recipe, such as Salmon Pasta Bake (recipe page 52), select pink-to-red colored Chinook (king), coho (silver) or sockeye (red) salmon. If appearance is not important, select the less expensive varieties of chum and pink salmon for recipes to make sandwiches, patties and loaves.

Using Cheese
● You'll get 2 cups shredded cheese from an 8-ounce package of semi-soft cheese, such as Cheddar, Swiss, mozzarella or Monterey Jack. Hard cheeses, such as Parmesan and Romano, are typically grated; 2 ounces of hard cheese will yield ½ cup grated.

Micro-thawing Vegetables
● When your recipe calls for thawed, frozen vegetables, rely on your microwave oven to thaw them in minutes. Use the defrost cycle, stopping every minute to loosen and break up the vegetables.

Using Garlic
● To easily remove the skin, lightly crush a garlic clove with the flat side of a wide kitchen knife to crack the skin. The skin will easily slip off.

● For those who prefer using garlic powder or bottled minced garlic, refer to this substitution guide: For 1 clove garlic use ⅛ teaspoon garlic powder or use ½ teaspoon bottled minced garlic.

Slicing Meat
● To make slicing raw meat easier, freeze chicken, turkey, beef or pork about 1 hour before cutting into thin strips.

Poultry Pointers
● The safest way to thaw frozen poultry is to defrost it in the refrigerator. Allow at least 24 hours for every 5 pounds of frozen poultry. Never thaw frozen poultry at room temperature. Try this quick method: Put the package of frozen poultry in a watertight plastic bag and submerge the bag in cold water. Change the water every 30 minutes until poultry is thawed. It will take 30 minutes to 1 hour to thaw 1 pound of frozen poultry.*

● If you don't have cooked chicken in the refrigerator, use cooked chicken from the supermarket deli. Or, cook your own chicken: Allow about 1 pound skinless, boneless raw chicken for 2 cups cubed cooked chicken.

● Use a sturdy plastic cutting board when cutting raw poultry instead of a wooden board. Since wood boards are porous, it is difficult to thoroughly wash them.

● When you shop, select chicken that is plump; that's a good indication it will be moist and meaty. Also look for poultry with skin that is clean, white to deep yellow in color and has no bruises or discolorations.

● The U.S. Department of Agriculture operates a toll-free Meat and Poultry Hot Line to answer your food safety questions about meat and poultry. From 10 a.m. to 4 p.m. Eastern Standard Time, Monday through Friday, home economists will answer your meat and poultry questions—just dial 1-800-535-4555. If you are in the Washington, DC, metropolitan area, dial (202) 447-3333.*

*Source: U.S. Department of Agriculture-Food Safety and Inspection Service.

Index

RECIPES BY SOUP